...IF YOU LIVED in THE DAYS OF THE KNIGHTS

BY Ann McGovern
ILLUSTRATED
BY Dan Andreasen

SCHOLASTIC INC.

NEW YORK   TORONTO   LONDON   AUCKLAND   SYDNEY
MEXICO CITY   NEW DELHI   HONG KONG

CONTENTS

When were the days of the knights?

Soldiers known as knights once dressed in armor and rode their horses into battle.

The days of the knights were a long time ago. This time in history is known as the Middle Ages, or medieval times. The Middle Ages lasted more than a thousand years, from about 400 to 1500. This book does not tell you about the entire Middle Ages. It tells you how you would have lived in England around the year 1250.

Highlights of the Middle Ages

780–1100	1096–1291	1150	1200	1455	1492
Vikings explore Europe and the New World	Crusades	First paper made in Europe	First universities — Oxford, England/ Paris, France/ Bologna, Italy	Gutenberg Bible/ first important book printed in Germany	Columbus sails to America

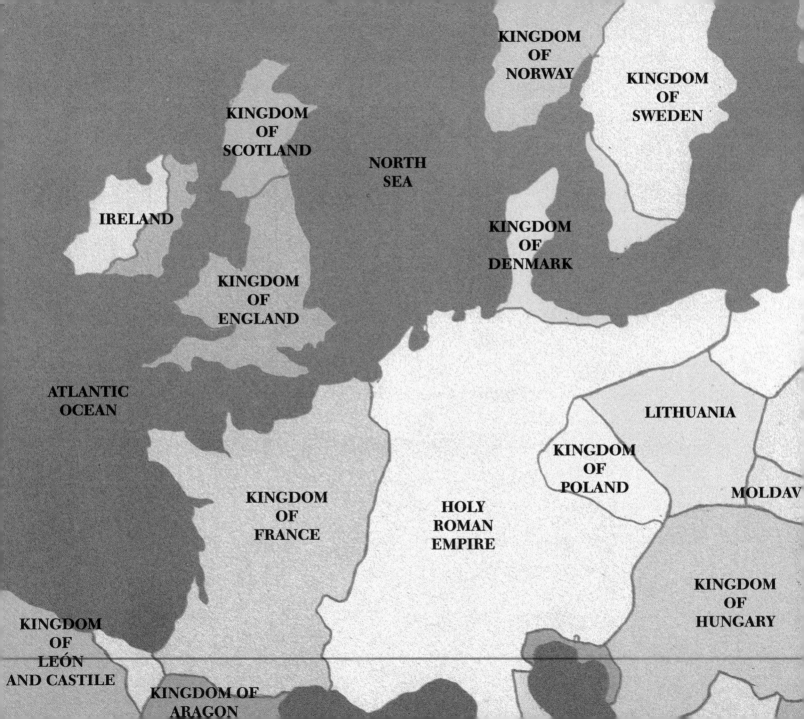

The way people lived in the Middle Ages was very different from how you live today. From the kind of bed you slept in to what you ate for breakfast; from the games you played to the clothes you wore; how you kept yourself clean, brushed your teeth, and went to the bathroom — everything about the Middle Ages would seem very strange to you today.

This map shows England and other kingdoms in northern Europe as they were around the year 1250.

Where did people live?

Most people lived in the country.

The kind of house you lived in depended on what kind of family you were born into.

In the Middle Ages, all the land in England belonged to the king. He gave parcels of land to nobles, such as barons and earls, who promised to support him. The nobles hired soldiers to fight battles for the king. These soldiers were knights.

The king, the nobles, and the knights did not farm the land. That work was done by peasants.

This system of land ownership is called the *feudal system*.

If you were the child of a king, you would live in a grand castle. Castles were forts in time of war as well as homes.

If your father was a baron or earl or other noble, you might live in a large manor house. Some rich nobles lived in castles. Some *very* rich nobles had more than one castle.

If your father was a knight, you might live in a good-sized house that had several rooms. Sometimes knights and their families lived in the noble's castle.

The Feudal System

THE
KING OF
ENGLAND

NOBLES
AND
BISHOPS
OF THE
CHURCH

KNIGHTS
AND
LESSER
NOBLES

PEASANTS

The feudal system was like a ladder. The king, at the top, owned all the land. The nobles ruled over the knights. The knights ruled over the peasants. The peasants were at the bottom. They ruled over no one.

If you were a peasant, you would live in a small cottage with one or two rooms.

Most peasant cottages were simply built and didn't last long. If your house began to fall apart, you'd build a new one. The old one would be used for farm equipment and to house animals.

Merchants who sold or made goods often lived in two-story homes. The ground floor was the workshop. You'd live on the second floor.

There were special places for men and women who belonged to religious orders: *Monks* lived in *monasteries*; *nuns* lived in *nunneries*.

What did people believe?

People believed in fairies and witches and devils. People thought that unicorns and dragons really lived.

Almost everybody was Catholic. The Church was very rich and powerful.

There were people, like the Jews, who worshiped God in different ways than Catholics. Jews who served the king were under his royal protection. But by 1290, the king had ordered all Jews to leave England.

In the Middle East, Muslims had their own way of worship. The Catholics called the Muslims "infidels," which means "no faith." The Crusades, a series of wars, were fought between Catholics and Muslims over who would control the Holy Land in the Middle East. Knights from Europe fought in these wars, which went on for two hundred years.

Some knights came home from the Crusades with new spices and silk fabrics. They brought back inventions like the wheelbarrow and new ideas about medicines.

Who could become a knight?

Not girls! Sons of knights became knights. Also, all the sons of nobles had to learn to be knights.

Being a knight was a great honor. It took many years of training.

Sometimes a peasant was made a knight. If a man showed great courage on the battlefield, he was made a knight right then and there as a reward.

How was a boy trained to be a knight?

At the age of seven or eight, a boy was sent away from his family. He went to live in the castle or manor house of a noble, who would be his "lord."

Your first job would be as a *page,* serving the lord and lady of the castle. You helped the lord get dressed in the morning. You waited on him at the table. You did all sorts of chores, like lighting the candles in the great hall of the castle. You learned to be a good chess player.

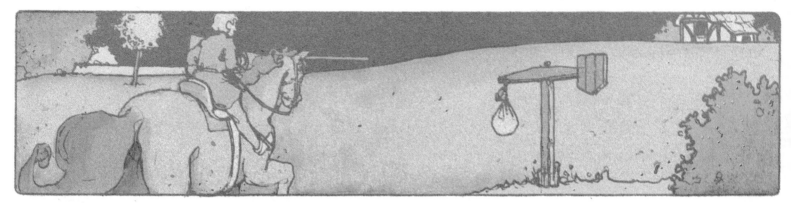

The quintain had a shield on one end of the crossbar and a sack of sand on the other. You would charge the shield with your lance. If you weren't quick enough, the sack of sand would swing around and knock you off your horse.

Most important, you learned to be a soldier. At first, you used a small wooden sword with a round shield called a *buckler.* You learned to ride a horse with one hand, so you could keep the other hand free for your weapon. You trained your horse to get used to the noise of battle. You fought in make-believe battles, sometimes with a *quintain.*

A knight needed to be strong. So you trained in wrestling, running, horsemanship, acrobatics, and sword fighting.

You learned reading and writing. From the ladies of the castle, you learned good manners, music, and dancing.

You learned to hunt.

When you turned eighteen, you were made a *squire*. You learned how to carve roasts and the correct way to serve wine. You looked after your lord's horses, his weapons, and his armor.

At twenty-one, you were finally ready to become a knight.

Was there a ceremony for a new knight?

You began by praying all night in church. In the morning, you took a bath as a sign that you were clean of body and spirit. You cut your hair to show that you honored God. Then you dressed in white clothes and a red robe. The color white stood for goodness and red meant that you would fight — even die — for the noble lord you served.

At sunrise, there was a church service. Your weapons and your armor were handed to you one at a time, each with a blessing by the priest.

You knelt before the noble who performed the *dubbing ceremony*. He tapped you on the neck with the side of his sword. That was supposed to be the only blow you would ever take without fighting back.

You swore to obey the knights' "code of chivalry" — to use your sword to defend the Church and protect widows, orphans, and the poor. And, most important, to serve your lord in battle.

Now you were a knight. If your name was Alfred, you would now be called *Sir* Alfred. Your wife would be called *Lady*.

The ceremony ended with a show of horsemanship and war games, followed by a great feast.

What did a castle look like?

A castle could hold a small army. Knights who lived in the castle had to be ready to fight in wars for their lords. Besides knights and their families, servants, and churchmen, many guests lived in the castle, too. Some guests stayed for years at a time.

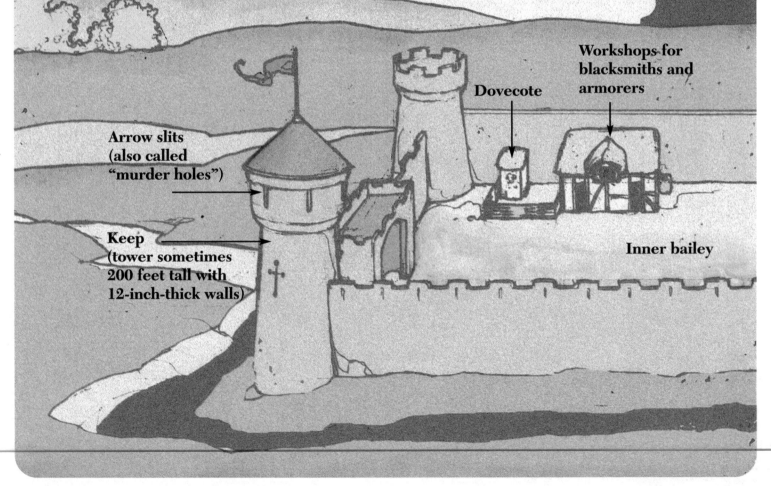

Dovecote

Workshops for blacksmiths and armorers

Arrow slits (also called "murder holes")

Keep (tower sometimes 200 feet tall with 12-inch-thick walls)

Inner bailey

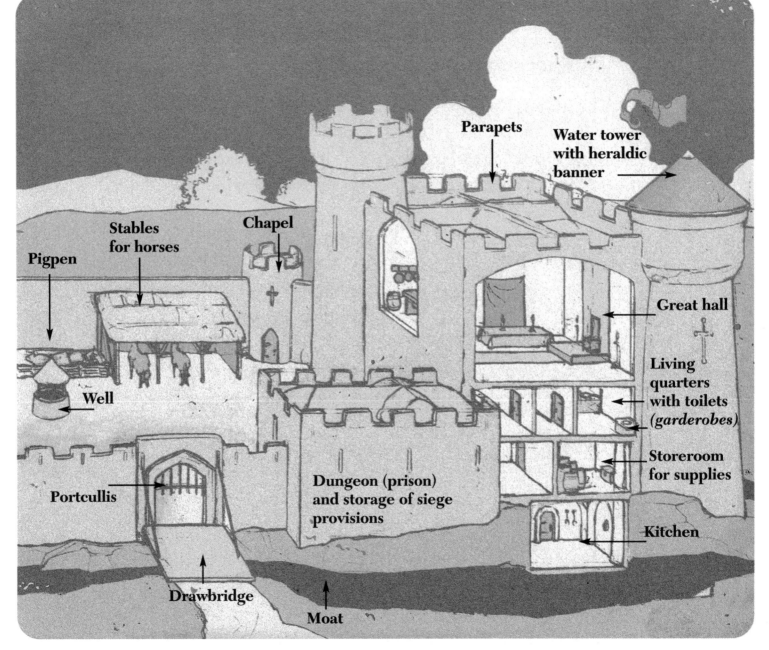

Parapets

Water tower with heraldic banner

Stables for horses

Chapel

Pigpen

Great hall

Well

Living quarters with toilets (garderobes)

Storeroom for supplies

Portcullis

Dungeon (prison) and storage of siege provisions

Kitchen

Drawbridge

Moat

What weapons were used in battle?

A knight's most important weapon was his sword. The most popular kind was the double-edge cutting sword. A knight might also hang a second great sword from his saddle.

Another important weapon was his *lance,* a long wooden spear tipped with steel.

Foot soldiers were not knights and didn't ride horses in battle. Many were peasants who were ordered to fight. Often, peasants did not even have armor to protect them. They fought on the ground with axes or bows and arrows and carried a round shield.

A soldier could shoot about ten arrows a minute. Sometimes he carried a spiked club to bash the enemy.

A *trebuchet* looked like a giant slingshot and could knock down the walls of a castle.

You didn't have to be strong to use a crossbow, like this one.

How did a knight get dressed for battle?

A knight got dressed from the bottom up. He sat down while his squire pulled on his leggings of *mail* over long leather stockings. He stood up while the thick cap and padded undergarment, called an *aketon,* were put on. Over that was his *hauberk,* the coat of mail that came down below his knees. It was made of up to 200,000 small iron rings that were linked together. Over the coat of mail came a cloth tunic to protect his armor from rusting. The rest of his outfit was buckled or strapped on.

A close-fitting *coif* of mail and the great *helm* — his heavy helmet over it — protected his neck and head. The helm had slits for seeing and holes for breathing.

It might take a squire fifteen minutes to dress a knight for battle.

A knight wouldn't be comfortable in his armor. His long-sleeved coat of mail alone weighed about twenty pounds. Add the chain-mail leggings, the great helm, and a shield. Everything together might weigh forty-five pounds. A knight had to be very fit to be able to run or get on his horse when he wore his full armor.

A knight would suffer in the heat. The sun made his helmet burning hot. With his helmet on, he couldn't scratch an itch or wipe away his sweat. He had trouble hearing or giving commands.

Later, knights wore armor made of solid metal plates instead of suits of chain mail. Even then, armor didn't always keep knights absolutely safe, especially against a weapon like the crossbow.

Armor could rust. To prevent rusting, a squire would put the knight's armor into a leather bag with vinegar and sand. Then he tossed the bag around so that the armor got a good washing.

What kind of horse did a knight ride?

He needed a horse that was heavy enough to handle the weight of his armor. The best horse was a white stallion.

A knight owned at least three horses. One for fighting, one for hunting, and one for *jousting* — a sport in which two knights fought with lances.

Horses needed to be protected, too. They wore head armor, called *shaffron,* on the battlefield.

How could you tell one knight from another?

By his *coat of arms.* Each knight had a different design on his shield that told people to which family he belonged. The same design appeared on the tunic he wore over his armor and on his helmet. Even the cloth that covered his horse was decorated with the family coat of arms.

Would you be comfortable in a castle?

Not in the winter. Castles were damp and very cold. The only warm place would be near the fireplaces. On the coldest days, even the drinking water in the castle's birdcages froze.

By 1250, most bedrooms had fireplaces. Fireplaces warmed the halls, too. Large tapestries, hanging on the walls, were decorations that helped keep out drafts.

Castles were dark. Small windows, covered with oiled cloth, did not let in much light. Kings and rich nobles had glass windows. So did churches.

Candles and torches were smoky and smelled bad, and there was always a danger of fire from the sparks.

You might not be comfortable at mealtimes, either. Chairs were only for nobles and special guests, who sat at the "high table." Everybody else sat on wooden benches and ate on long boards called *trestle tables*. The floor was covered with straw that got dirty from spilled food and dog poop. New straw was sprinkled with sweet-smelling herbs to hide the bad smells.

What kinds of clothes did people wear?

Children didn't have special clothes. They wore the same styles as their parents. Babies were *swaddled* — wrapped up tightly in strips of linen cloth. As soon as babies began to walk, they were dressed in loose smocks.

When knights weren't in armor, they wore brightly dyed clothes made of fine wool, silk, or velvet, trimmed with fur. In winter, knights wore fur-lined jackets under their tunics and warm cloaks. They wore colored tights called *hose,* held in place by *garters* at the knee, and pointed leather shoes. Outdoors they wore boots, often the same color as their cloaks. There were no pockets, so men and women wore purses that slid over their belts.

Merchants wore tunics over their hose. In hot weather, they rolled the hose down.

Women loved bright colors and fine fabrics, too. Their long gowns, called *kirtles,* lasted a lifetime and were often handed down to their daughters. Long sleeves could be taken off and sewn back on. Tunics were often *reversible* and could be worn either side out.

Women wore silver and ivory ornaments in their hair. Gold dust made their hair sparkle.

Girls wore their hair loose. Their mothers wore their hair in braids coiled around their ears. The hair was covered with a veil or a band of linen that went under the chin. On top of this went a small, round hat with a wide brim.

Both men and women loved to show off their jewels. They even wore their rings *over* their gloves.

Women and children wore tunics over their dresses, too.

Peasants often made their own clothes out of rough cloth. In winter, peasants wore sheepskin cloaks. Women wrapped their woolen hoods around their heads like turbans. For working outdoors, they wore shorter tunics and heavy boots and gloves.

Peasants sometimes wore clothes that knights and their families no longer wanted.

What did you wear to sleep? Nothing. Under their covers, people slept naked.

Clothing fashions changed quickly, just as they do today — but only for the rich. Peasant clothing stayed much the same.

How did you keep your clothes clean?

It was hard. Candle wax dripped on them; gravy and wine got spilled on them.

Before you put your clothes away in wooden chests, they had to be shaken and brushed, laid in the sun, and sprinkled with nice-smelling herbs.

What furniture did people have?

They didn't have much, even in castles. A lord and his lady slept on a bed with a wooden frame. They had a soft padded or feather mattress, pillows, blankets, and linen sheets. Curtains hung around the bed for privacy and warmth.

Big chests were used for storing clothes, household goods, and valuables, and were locked up. There were no closets. Sometimes clothes were hung on poles, safely away from rats.

The only chairs with backs and armrests were for nobles. Everyone else sat on benches, stools, or on the straw-covered floor.

Most houses had a trestle table — just a board that rested on wooden supports.

There were no mechanical clocks in England until the late 1200s. People told time with sundials, but sundials

didn't work on cloudy days. There were water clocks, too. In the summer, the water might dry up and in the winter, the drops of water might freeze. So no one ever knew the exact time.

Where did people sleep?

The big bedroom in a castle was called a *solar*. Babies in cradles shared their parents' room. So did the family's favorite dogs. Children and servants slept in the solar, too, often on straw-filled *pallets* on the floor. By day, the pallets were rolled up and stored away, like sleeping bags.

A merchant's house had a smaller solar. Sometimes people slept on the shop floor.

Many peasants had only one room. The whole family might have slept there.

How did people keep clean?

It wasn't easy for peasants. They had no running water.

Servants or pages in the castle brought their lords hot water in a basin every morning for washing up.

On each floor was a sink for washing up. The water came through pipes from a tank on the top of the castle.

You cleaned your teeth with a twig, or you wiped them with a cloth.

People who study the Middle Ages don't agree about how often people bathed. Some say they seldom took baths. Others say they bathed often and loved to soak in a wooden tub for a long time.

Soap was made at home, but it was smelly. To make your bath smell good, you'd sprinkle herbs and flowers in the bath water.

Some people didn't take baths at home. They went to public bathhouses called *stews*. Some bathed in rivers and streams.

What did people do about garbage?

People dumped their garbage outside. Sometimes they carried bunches of herbs and flowers to sniff out of doors because of the bad smell.

You were used to bad smells. You were used to fleas biting you. You were used to finding lice on your body and bugs in your food. But rats were the worst! There were rats running around everywhere, even in the finest castles. They carried germs that made people sick.

Were there bathrooms?

Most castles didn't have a separate room for bathing and washing up.

The toilets, called *garderobes*, were usually built high up in the thick walls. A garderobe was just a plank with a hole in it. The stuff went down a chute that ended in a pit far below. The smelly pit was cleaned out often — but not often enough!

People also used pots for toilets. Sometimes they dumped the smelly pots into the street without warning.

There was no toilet paper. Instead, people used curved wooden sticks or hay.

Did people work hard?

Peasants worked from sunrise to sundown, farming and caring for livestock.

More than half the peasants were *serfs*. The serfs had to farm the lord's land. In return, they got some land and a house for their own families.

The law said that serfs were bound to the lord of the manor. They were not allowed to leave the land, and the lord could not make them go. But, in fact, serfs bought and sold property — even land. Serfs who managed to make enough money could buy their freedom. Some became free by marrying a free person or by running away.

Free or serf, a peasant worked hard. So did everyone in his family.

In the fall, you plowed the fields and collected dead branches for firewood, hunted animals for food, threshed corn, gathered nuts, and made wine.

In the winter, you planted wheat, repaired your houses, and made tools.

In the spring, you planted oats and barley.

In the summer, you sheared the sheep, harvested crops, cut and stored the hay, and collected honey from the beehives.

Did children work?

The children of merchants helped their parents by selling wares and cleaning the shop.

Even the children of nobles and knights worked. Girls helped with spinning and other chores. Boys trained to be knights.

Some boys were sent away from home to learn a trade from an expert. At the age of fourteen, a child could become an *apprentice* to a master who taught him everything he knew about his trade or craft. You might learn to become a stonecutter, a tailor, a carpenter, or a metal worker.

You would live in the master's house. At the end of seven years of hard work, you would be ready to take an exam. If you passed, you would be called a *journeyman*. You would be free to work in another shop if you wanted to.

If you were very good at your work, you could become a master and open your own shop. First, you had to make a *masterpiece* to show your skill.

Who worked in the castle?

If the lord of the castle was very rich, he might have hundreds of people working for him.

Knights served as soldiers and defended the castle in war. *Porters* guarded outside doors. *Watchmen* made sure all was well.

Pig boys took care of the pigs in the pigpens. Another boy made sure birds didn't eat newly planted seeds. His job was to throw sticks and stones at the birds to keep them away.

There were *huntsmen* in charge of hunts and *grooms* in charge of horses. *Scurries* made spurs for the horses.

A *keeper of the wardrobe* took care of the clothing and made sure the tailors were doing a good job. *Laundresses* washed the sheets, towels, and tablecloths.

Kitchen boys and *kitchen maids* worked in the kitchen, buttery, and pantry. A *dresser* arranged food on platters, a *saucer* made the sauces, a *brewer* brewed the ale or cider, and a *waverer* washed the hands of people dining at the high table.

There were also *bakers, wafer makers, chandlers* who made candles, a *trumpeter* to announce dinner, and an *almoner* who gave out alms — leftover food — to the poor.

The *steward* was in charge of the lord's entire estate and all its servants. *Cofferers* guarded chests filled with treasures. *Clerks* helped run the business of the castle.

A *chaplain* was in charge of the chapel.

Many people worked at entertaining noble families — *acrobats, jesters, jugglers, magicians, minstrels, musicians, actors,* and *dancers.*

What were girls taught?

Some girls were taught to read and write. Many daughters of nobles went to live in another castle when they were eight. They learned to dance and play a musical instrument. They took bugs out of the wool before it was spun into thread.

A noblewoman learned how to manage a castle and how to defend the castle if it was attacked when her husband was away. She was in charge of hiring the servants, choosing the wines, planting a kitchen garden, and treating illnesses with herbs.

If you were the daughter of a merchant, you might help in your father's shop. If you had younger brothers and sisters, you would help your mother care for them.

Daughters of peasants worked in the fields. They helped their mothers bake, brew beer, raise ducks and geese, and milk the cows.

Were your parents strict?

Yes. If you didn't obey, watch out! Boys were beaten to "get the devil out of them." Girls who didn't follow the strict rules of behavior could be punished for things like laughing too loudly, getting a sunburn, or wearing boys' clothes.

What did people do for fun?

Children played with toys. Poor families made their own toys — hobbyhorses, dolls, tops, and hoops. Knights and nobles bought toys for their children at the big fairs or had them custom-made by the town toy maker or carpenter.

There were games of hoodman's buff (we call it blind-man's buff today) and walking on logs. People played checkers and chess.

Noblemen and noblewomen loved hunting, especially with *falcons,* the special birds they trained to catch prey.

In winter, there were snowball fights. When the rivers and ponds froze, men and boys went ice-skating on skates made from horses' shinbones. The polished bones were tied onto their shoes.

Boys played at making war. Girls played with dolls.

People kept birds in cages, and some families had pet dogs.

Boys played archery and a kind of hockey. Football was different from the sport played today. There were no rules for this rough game, and players could get badly hurt. The football was a pig's bladder covered with leather. Boys chased after the round ball, knocking over anyone in their way.

Most people didn't have books to read, but everyone loved telling and listening to old folktales. A few rich households owned the *Book of Saints*. It told how Catholic saints lived and died and what lessons might be learned from their lives.

After dinner, there were plays, music, and dancing. Some knights were also musicians, called *troubadours*.

Everyone celebrated holidays and festivals. They had fun at the great fairs, where acrobats walked on stilts and tame bears danced.

There were plenty of jousts and tournaments where knights could show off. The goal in jousting was for one knight to knock the other knight off his horse with his lance. In tournaments, knights used swords. The winner got to take the defeated knight's horse and armor.

Where did people buy and sell their clothes and food?

At markets and great fairs. People came from far away to buy, sell, or trade goods they made and food they had grown.

Some people bought cloth and trimmings at a merchant's shop or at a fair. They gave the cloth to a tailor, who then made their clothes.

What happened to people who broke the law?

A baker who sold stale bread had to wear a piece of moldy bread on a string around his neck. If someone sold spoiled fish, he was made to wear the smelly, rotten fish. A wine seller who sold bad wine had to drink some of it. The rest was poured over his head.

People were not allowed to do any work on Sunday or on feast days. If they were caught working, they were whipped.

If a knight committed a crime, he had to give up his armor. Then he was tied up and pulled through the streets of the town in a wagon so that everyone could know he had done something wrong.

A thief who didn't steal much might have a hand cut off. But a thief who stole something *really* valuable was hanged. Hanging was the most serious punishment. Anyone more than twelve years old could be hanged.

The poor were allowed to beg, but others who begged could be beaten or put in the *stocks* — a wooden seat with holes that trapped the legs. People passing by might laugh at you or throw garbage. Women could be put into the stocks for scolding their husbands or neighbors.

Would you go to school?

Not many children went to school. If a girl wanted to be a nun, she might be sent to a school run by a nunnery. Most people thought girls only needed to learn how to run a household. But some girls were taught to read and write anyhow.

Some of the sons of nobles or knights were taught reading and writing by tutors or priests who lived at the castle.

Boys who wanted to become priests went to church schools. Some went to "song schools," where they learned to read and sing chants and hymns in Latin. You needed to know Latin to be a clerk in government or in the church.

All the lessons were in Latin. If you forgot your Latin, the master might say: "*vae natibus,*" which is Latin for "woe to the buttocks." Then he'd give you a beating on your backside with a bunch of sticks.

Your teacher also had a *palmer* — a stick with a flat wooden disk at the end. It was used for swatting the palms of boys who didn't behave.

You wouldn't have your own desk. You would share a bench with other boys or sit on the straw-covered floor.

How would you learn?

You wouldn't have schoolbooks. Your teacher had the only book. He would read aloud out of his book. Then the students would repeat the words. You would do this over and over until you could say your lessons by heart.

You practiced writing on a slate with chalk, or on a piece of wood coated with green or black wax, using a stylus of bone, ivory, or metal.

Peasant children didn't go to school. They were too busy working.

How were books made?

Every book was made by hand. People who made books were called *scribes*. They used parchment paper and pens made from goose feathers. Each book could take months to make, especially if it had illustrations. It would take a scribe over a year to make one Bible.

Some books were works of art, with brightly colored pictures sometimes decorated with gold leaf. Books were so valuable they were not kept on shelves, but were locked away in chests. A student could borrow or rent a book, but he had to be very careful not to damage it or lose it.

How did you get around?

You'd be very uncomfortable when you traveled on the roads. Gravel and dirt roads were bumpy and full of holes. When it rained, the roads were muddy and you could get stuck.

Roads were crowded with horses, carts, and mules. A merchant going to market might have as many as seventy mules or horses to carry his wares. Flocks of sheep and cattle going to market shared the road with wandering minstrels, actors, musicians, monks, nuns, and robbers.

A rich baron with more than one castle might move from one to another, sometimes with up to one hundred servants, one hundred knights, and one hundred horses. Behind them were carts, packhorses, and mules carrying household treasures.

Everyone on the road faced the danger of robbers, wolves, and bears. People sent their goods on boats if they could. Even then, they had to watch out for pirates and sudden bad storms.

Where did people sleep when they traveled?

Nobles, knights, and their families slept in the nearest castle. Merchants slept in crowded, dirty inns. A bed was shared by as many people as could fit in it. Food was bad, bugs crawled everywhere, and there were rats.

Everyone, including peasants, traveled to markets. They usually could get there and back in a single day.

Sometimes people made religious journeys, called *pilgrimages.* It could take more than a week to reach the holy place.

What happened if you got sick?

Medicines were made at home from herbs and plants. They were supposed to cure almost anything, from a cold to a serious disease.

Herbs were crushed, ground, boiled, and strained. Sometimes herbs were mixed with worms, animal fat, blood, garlic, bits of bone — even fingernails.

To find a cure, your mother might look in her book of doctoring that had been handed down to her by her mother. Some popular remedies were:

- *For a skin rash — rub with goose fat*

- *For boils on your skin — rub with a mixture of goose fat and garlic*

- *To fade freckles — rub with blood from a bull or a rabbit*

- *For a sore throat — drink a tea made from black-berry leaves*

- *To heal a bruise — bathe the bruise twice a day in a bowl of water heated with a hot stone*

People also believed that magic spells could make you better. They believed that the devil could make you sick. So could bad smells.

If herbal mixes and magic didn't cure you, you might
have to be bled. A vein in your arm would be cut open to
let some blood flow out. Sometimes leeches were put on
your skin to suck the bad blood out.

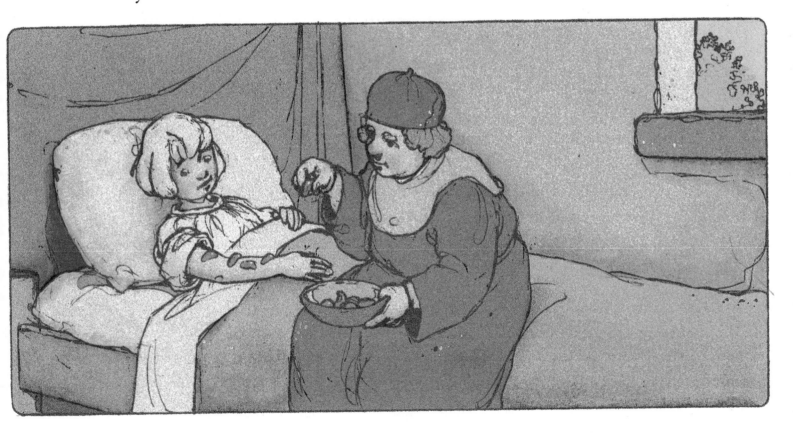

Were there doctors and hospitals?

There were only a few doctors and mostly they treated rich people. Some of the doctors were women.

Hospitals were set up by the church. There were four hundred hospitals in England in the year 1250. Everybody was welcome except those who showed up with hunting dogs and hawks.

You would get gentle care. Your clothes would be cleaned of lice. You would get baths often. But when the hospital was crowded, you might have to share your bed with another sick person.

Operations were dangerous and painful. The person having the operation had to be chained to the operating table so he couldn't move. There were no anesthetics or painkillers. Operating instruments weren't very clean, so there was a good chance of getting infections. Still, some people survived thanks to the operation.

If you needed a tooth pulled, you'd go to the town barber.

If you needed to have a mole removed, you'd go to the town barber.

If you needed a bloodletting, you'd go to the town barber.

Some days, barbers didn't have much time to cut hair.

What did people eat?

Breakfast in the great hall of a castle would be an early snack after morning church. The rich were served white bread with a slice of cold meat or cheese. Peasants ate a coarse, dark bread made from barley, wheat, and rye flour.

Dinner was the main meal of the day. You ate as early as ten in the morning, and the meal could last till afternoon. On holidays and feasts more than ten courses were served. The celebrations didn't end until dark.

People had fresh meat to eat in the spring and summer. They salted and smoked some of it so that it would keep during winter months.

Most nobles ate meat that was boiled or roasted on a spit or made into stews. Only the rich could buy raisins and spices. Spices were so valuable they were kept locked up.

Castles had their own fishponds.

At a feast, the squires and cooks paraded around the Great Hall, showing off the different dishes.

Every kind of bird was cooked — storks, starlings, even vultures. It was a treat to have whole pigeons or peacocks in a raisin sauce. Or a wild boar complete with its tusks! A peacock might be stuffed and roasted. Then its tail feathers would be stuck back on as decoration when it was served.

Fresh fruits were a rare treat. Peasants would make special gifts of fresh berries and cherries for their lords and ladies. Sweets weren't for the end of the meals. Between the meat dishes, you might eat apple tarts or custard.

Peasants made bacon and pork pies. They made bread mixed with peas or beans. They ate porridge and cheese, grew cabbages and onions, and kept hens for eggs. They used herbs in their cooking. They sweetened their food with honey.

Everyone — even children — drank ale or wine and homemade cider. It wasn't safe to drink plain water — it was full of germs that could make you sick.

What kinds of dishes would you use?

Your plate was a piece of day-old bread. It was shared by two people. If you had any bread left at the end of the meal, it would be given to the poor. It was bad manners to eat the plate of bread.

You would share a cup with the person next to you. To be polite, you wiped the rim after you drank. Guests were given spoons, but they had to bring their own knives. There were no such things as forks!

Did you have to think about manners?

You were not to gnaw on bones or poke your fingers into eggs or butter your bread with your thumbs. No spitting across the table or wiping your teeth or your knife on the tablecloth. No drinking from a shared cup with greasy lips.

Your dog could come to meals, but it was bad manners to scratch your pet. If you used your hand to blow your nose, you had to wipe your hand on your shirt.

Even in war, knights were expected to have good manners. No attacking an unarmed man. No fair for two knights to fight against one. No hitting below the belt or kicking a knight when he's down. Many knights didn't pay attention to these rules.

How was Christmas celebrated in the castle?

You began by celebrating Christmas on Christmas Eve. The holiday lasted twelve days. Every day there was another celebration.

The castle was decorated with holly, ivy, and other greens. A huge piece of tree trunk was brought inside and put on the hearth. This "Yule log" burned throughout the twelve days.

On the Twelfth Day of Christmas, a special cake was baked with a bean and a pea inside it. Whoever found the bean played the King. Whoever found the pea was the Queen. They led the dancing and acting.

At Christmastime, the king gave expensive gifts to his knights — robes and jewels.

How did you celebrate your birthday and other special days?

If you were the child of a noble, your birthday celebration began in the castle before noon and lasted till dark. Musicians, jugglers, and tumblers entertained you and your guests. Magicians pulled roses from your ear. There might be so many guests that some of them would have to sit on the floor.

You would celebrate many *holy days*. (Later those words became "holiday.") There were more than one hundred holy days in the Catholic calendar every year.

Saint Valentine's Day was February 14th, and you ate heart-shaped cakes at the feast. Valentine cards had not been invented yet.

May 1st was May Day. A May Queen was chosen, people danced around a "maypole," and girls made flowery wreaths for their hair.

How old were girls and boys when they got married?

Today people live long lives. Many celebrate their one hundredth birthday. But that wasn't true in the Middle Ages. Most people didn't live past the age of fifty. So girls and boys who wanted to have a family got married young, often by age sixteen.

Girls could not choose who they would marry. Marriages were not for love. They were more of a business arrangement. A knight often got more land and riches when he arranged a marriage between his daughter and the son of another knight.

What was a wedding like in the Middle Ages?

In some ways, it was like a wedding today. The wedding took place at the church door. The bridegroom gave his bride a ring. They shared a piece of bread and a sip of wine.

After the church ceremony, the guests threw seeds to show they hoped the couple would have many children.

If the wedding party was at the manor house or in a castle, the great hall was richly decorated. Sweet-smelling mint and heather were sprinkled on the straw-covered floor. Linen cloths covered the tables. Silver- and gold-trimmed goblets and the best candlesticks were taken out of the chests, where they were kept under lock and key.

After a huge feast, every man danced with the bride.
People sang, and musicians played on their lutes, harps,
pipes, and drums.

Are there knights today?

The days of the knights ended in England about five hundred years ago. But today, the queen of England awards knighthoods to Englishmen and Englishwomen who make extraordinary contributions to their country. Knights today are not nobles or soldiers. They are actors, scientists, schoolteachers, and great leaders in their fields.

There is still a dubbing ceremony today, but it is not as fancy as in the Middle Ages. The person being honored kneels on a stool in front of the queen, who taps the new knight on the shoulders with the blade of a sword. Afterward, the knight receives a star or a badge — a symbol of his new status. A man can now use the title *Sir* before his name. A woman knight has the title *Dame*.

Foreigners sometimes receive an honorary knighthood, but only English knights can be called "Sir" or "Dame."

How do we know about life in the Middle Ages?

Historians — people who study the past — use many clues to solve the mystery of how people lived long ago.

To learn about the Middle Ages, historians study paintings, tapestries, and stained-glass windows that were made in that period. They look at tools, weapons, and armor. They examine manuscripts, documents, and books.

Many castles and cathedrals that were built during medieval times are still standing in Europe. Some are in very bad shape. But by studying paintings and records from the time, historians can tell what the buildings looked like in the year 1250.

Different records were kept during the Middle Ages. They tell about the church, town government, marriages, and even how people died and what land was left to their family.

Old manuscripts show what people ate, what songs were sung, which herbs were used for treating the sick, and many other details of everyday life. All of these clues help give us an idea of how it must have been to live in the days of the knights.

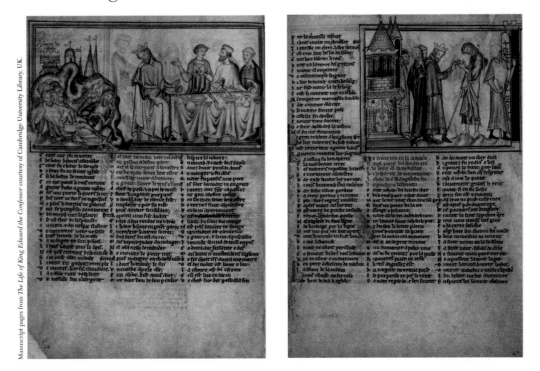

These pages are from a kind of book called an illuminated manuscript. "Illuminated" means that the manuscript has pictures. The book was made around the year 1250. Books like this tell us a lot about what life was like 750 years ago.

GLOSSARY

aketon (say AK-tun) A knee-length padded *tunic* worn by a knight under his *chain mail*.

almoner A person who gives money, food, or other gifts to the poor.

apprentice A boy who is learning a trade.

buckler A small round shield worn on the arm.

chain mail Garments made of many small, linked iron rings and used as armor.

chandler A person who makes candles.

chaplain The priest in charge of the castle's chapel, a small church.

coat of arms A design that stands for a particular *noble* family and used to decorate items such as shields, banners, and helmets that knights used in battle or in *tournaments*.

code of chivalry (SHIV-ul-ree) Rules of etiquette that knights were supposed to follow in their behavior toward women.

cofferer (KOFF-er-er) A person in the castle who is in charge of the chest (or "coffer") where valuables are kept.

coif (KWAF) A cap made of *chain mail* that was worn underneath the knight's helmet.

crossbow A weapon with a spring trigger for firing arrows.

Crusades The Christian military expeditions that occurred between 1096 and 1270 with the purpose of taking the Holy Land away from the Muslims. The Holy Land is the area in which Christians believed that Christ lived and worked — mostly modern Israel.

dovecote A small house built on a platform used for raising pigeons (doves).

dubbing ceremony The service at which a *squire* becomes a knight.

falcon A kind of hawk trained to help human hunters.

feudal system A kind of political and social organization based on land ownership that was used in Europe from the ninth to the fifteenth centuries.

garderobe (GARD-robe) Toilet. The word comes from

two French words — *garde*, meaning save, and *robe*, meaning clothes. People thought the smell from the toilets helped keep away moths that damaged clothes.

hauberk (HO-burk) The coat of *chain mail* that protected the knight's arms, chest, back, and knees.

helm A heavy iron helmet that completely covered the head.

hoodman's buff A game similar to blindman's buff.

inner bailey A courtyard inside the castle walls.

journeyman A person who has learned a trade; achieved after seven years as an *apprentice*.

jousting A contest at *tournaments* between two knights on horseback using *lances*.

keep A tall round or rectangular tower; the strongest and most secure part of a castle.

kirtle (KER-tle) A long dress worn by women and girls.

lance A long wooden shaft fitted with a pointed steel head; a weapon used by a knight on horseback.

mail (see chain mail)

master A person who has become an expert in a trade.

minstrel A musical entertainer. Minstrels who travel from place to place are called *wandering minstrels*.

monastery A building or group of buildings housing monks, men of a religious order.

noble A person of title (such as a baron or earl) who owns land and serves a king.

nunnery A building or group of buildings housing women who serve the church as nuns.

page A boy aged 8 to 17 in training to be a knight.

pallet A straw-filled sack used as a mattress, usually laid directly on the floor like a sleeping bag.

palmer A stick with a flat wooden disk at one end used to slap the palms of children who misbehaved.

pilgrimage A journey to worship at a holy place.

portcullis (PORT-kul-iss) A heavy iron gate hung over the castle doorway. The gate can be lowered to keep people out.

quintain A post with a swinging crosspiece used to practice charging with a *lance*.

scribe A person who writes out all the words in a book.

scurries (singular: scurry) Workers at the castle who make spurs for the horses.

serf A peasant working for the benefit of a *noble*.

shaffron A hood that fits over a horse's head and protects it in battle.

solar The room in a castle where the family sleeps or relaxes.

squire A boy age 18 to 21 in training to be a knight.

stew A public bathhouse.

stocks A wooden frame that locks a person's feet in place; used as a punishment for minor crimes.

stylus A short rod made of bone, ivory, or metal used like a pencil; for writing on a *wax tablet*.

tapestry A large hand-woven wall-hanging with a pattern or picture; used for decoration and for insulation against the cold.

tournament An event featuring *jousting* and other contests displaying a knight's skills.

trebuchet (TREB-oo-shay) A catapult with weights to pull down the arm and a long sling for tossing rocks or other missiles over the walls of a castle.

trestle table A long wooden table made up of a board placed over two or more triangular supports called trestles.

troubadour (TROOB-a-door) A person who sings and plays a musical instrument.

tunic A garment with straight sides worn over a *kirtle* or other garment.

wax tablet A rectangular frame covered with soft wax used for writing on, like a slate.

In memory of my friend and mentor,
Beatrice Schenk de Regniers

ACKNOWLEDGMENTS

Once again, I am grateful for the generous assistance and resources of New York City's public libraries. A special thanks to Barbara A. Hanawalt, King George III Professor of British History at Ohio State University, for reviewing the manuscript.

ISBN 0-439-10565-X

Art direction by Ursula S. Albano • Book design by Christopher Motil

15 14 13

7 8 9/0

Printed in the U.S.A.
First Scholastic printing, March 2001